STEM *trailblazer* BIOS

ASTRONAUT AND
PHYSICIST
SALLY RIDE

MARGARET J. GOLDSTEIN

Lerner Publications ◆ Minneapolis

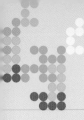

Lerner Publications Company
A division of Lerner Publishing Group, Inc.
241 First Avenue North
Minneapolis, MN 55401 USA

For reading levels and more information, look up this title at www.lernerbooks.com.

Library of Congress Cataloging-in-Publication Data

Names: Goldstein, Margaret J., author.
Title: Astronaut and physicist Sally Ride / Margaret J. Goldstein.
Description: Minneapolis : Lerner Publications, [2018] | Series: STEM trailblazer bios | Audience: Ages 7–11. | Audience: Grades 4 to 6. |
Includes bibliographical references and index.
Identifiers: LCCN 2017018464 (print) | LCCN 2017024973 (ebook) | ISBN 9781541500105 (eb pdf) | ISBN 9781541500099 (lb : alk. paper) | ISBN 9781541512177 (pb : alk. paper)
Subjects: LCSH: Ride, Sally—Juvenile literature. | United States. National Aeronautics and Space Administration—Biography—Juvenile literature. | Women astronauts—United States—Biography—Juvenile literature. | Astronauts—United States—Biography—Juvenile literature. | Women physicists—United States—Biography—Juvenile literature. | Physicists—United States—Biography—Juvenile literature.
Classification: LCC TL789.85.R53 (print) | LCC TL789.85.R53 G64 2018 (ebook) | DDC 629.45/0092 [[B]]—dc23

LC record available at https://lccn.loc.gov/2017018464

Manufactured in the United States of America
1-43644-33461-7/5/2017

The images in this book are used with the permission of: Michael Rougier/The LIFE Picture Collection/Getty Images, p. 4; Aviation History Collection/Alamy Stock Photo, p. 5; Seth Poppel Yearbook Library, p. 6; Andrea Izzotti/Shutterstock.com, p. 7; Courtesy Tam O'Shaughnessy, p. 8; ©b r e n t/flickr.com (CC BY 2.0), p. 9; Jim Heaphy/Wikimedia Commons (CC BY-SA 3.0), p. 10; Chuck Painter/Stanford News Service, p. 11; NASA/JSC, pp. 12, 14, 15, 17, 21, 22, 23, 25, 27; SPUTNIK/Alamy Stock Photo, p. 16; AP Photo, p. 19; YURI GRIPAS/REUTERS/Newscom, p. 24.

Front cover: NASA/JSC.

Main body text set in Adrianna Regular 13/22. Typeface provided by Chank.

CONTENTS

Chapter 1

Astronaut John Glenn's family watches his 1962 space launch on TV.

BLAST OFF!

February 20, 1962, was an exciting day for the United States. That's when astronaut John Glenn climbed into a small space capsule in Florida, and huge rockets blasted him into space. He became the first American to **orbit** Earth. Millions of Americans watched the launch on TV.

In Los Angeles, California, Sally Ride was watching too. Her teacher at Encino Elementary School had wheeled a black-and-white TV set into her classroom so the students could watch the launch.

Sally was in sixth grade. She didn't know what her future would hold. She didn't know that she too would become an astronaut—and the first American woman to fly in space.

Ride stands in her flight suit before her first launch into space in 1983.

Sally poses for a high school yearbook photo in 1968.

STUDYING SCIENCE

Sally was born on May 26, 1951. Her parents, Dale and Joyce Ride, always encouraged Sally and her sister, Karen, to work hard and pursue their interests. Sally became interested in science when she was in junior high school. She subscribed to *Scientific American* magazine, and her parents bought her a telescope. From her front lawn, Sally could look through the telescope for close-up views of planets and constellations, or groups of stars, in the night sky.

Sally attended a private high school in Los Angeles called Westlake School for Girls. A science teacher there, Elizabeth Mommaerts, encouraged Sally's passion for science. During her senior year, Sally took an introductory physics class at the University of California, Los Angeles (UCLA). But an English teacher at Westlake was less supportive. She told her class that Sally had "a first-rate mind, wasted in science."

Sally ignored the English teacher. She wanted to study physics in college. She was especially interested in **astrophysics**. Astrophysics deals with the properties and behavior of objects in space such as stars, planets, and solar systems. At the time, Sally did not think about becoming an astronaut. Rather, she was fascinated by space and interested in knowing more about what existed beyond Earth. Sally decided to study physics at Swarthmore College, a small school in Pennsylvania.

Swarthmore College

Chapter 2

Sally loved tennis and played competitively in high school and college

TRAJECTORY

At Swarthmore, Sally also played tennis. She'd begun playing as a child, and by the time she graduated from high school, she was a top-ranked tennis player among girls her age in the United States. On the Swarthmore tennis team, she dominated the competition, winning the Eastern Intercollegiate Women's Singles Championship.

But Sally missed the warm weather in Southern California. She was more serious about tennis than ever, and she knew in California she could play tennis outdoors all year. She even thought she might become a professional tennis player. So she quit Swarthmore after three semesters and returned to Los Angeles.

She enrolled at UCLA and joined the school's tennis team, but her dream of turning pro was short-lived. "I realized finally and for certain . . . that my education, science, was more important to me than tennis was," she said. But tennis taught Sally self-control and discipline, traits that would serve her well in the future.

UCLA campus

The
Physics
and Astrophysics
Building at Stanford
University, where
Ride studied for
several years

HITTING THE BOOKS

Ride recommitted herself to science. For her junior year,
she transferred from UCLA to Stanford University in Palo
Alto, California. She was one of very few women in the
Physics Department.

After earning her bachelor's degree, Ride stayed at Stanford for graduate school. She earned a master's degree in physics and then began working on a PhD in astrophysics. She studied how tiny particles called electrons behave as they speed through outer space. She also studied how waves of energy called X-rays interact with gases surrounding stars.

Ride works on a project at Stanford.

REACH FOR THE STARS

In January 1977, Ride saw an announcement in the Stanford University newspaper saying that the National Aeronautics and Space Administration (NASA) was recruiting female astronauts. NASA runs the US space program. Previously, NASA had trained only men to become astronauts. The first astronauts were military airplane pilots. But NASA wanted women to join the program, and they didn't have to be pilots to apply. The agency planned to send both pilots and scientists into orbit on its new fleet of **space shuttles**. The astronaut-scientists, called mission specialists, would help operate the shuttle, study Earth and its **atmosphere**, and conduct experiments to understand how **weightlessness** affects living things.

NASA's first group of astronauts was chosen in 1959. All seven men were military pilots.

When Ride saw the notice in the newspaper, she knew that she wanted to go to space. She wrote to NASA, which sent her a formal application.

More than eight thousand people applied for the astronaut program that year. After medical tests, fitness tests, and interviews, the agency selected thirty-five astronaut trainees. Ride was one of six women in the group.

In June 1978, Ride finished her PhD in astrophysics. The next month, she moved to Houston, Texas, to begin astronaut training at the Johnson Space Center.

Chapter 3

Ride prepares to take off in a jet before her first spaceflight.

DANGER

EJECTION SEAT

A WOMAN'S PLACE IS IN SPACE

Ride studied medicine, oceanography, geology, and other sciences at the Johnson Space Center. She learned about the space shuttle's electronics, engines, and fuel supply. She practiced jumping from airplanes with parachutes. She also learned to fly jets.

BEHIND THE SCENES

When they are not in space, astronauts do jobs on the ground. Ride helped test the space shuttle's robotic arm. It was a giant crane that astronauts would use to launch new **satellites** and to capture old ones. Ride learned to work the levers that controlled the arm's movement. She documented problems in its operation and worked with engineers to solve them.

In April 1981, *Columbia* was the first shuttle to fly in space. During *Columbia*'s second and third flights, Ride worked on the ground as a capsule communicator. She spoke to the

Ride speaks to the crew of *Columbia* during a test before the shuttle's second flight.

shuttle astronauts on the radio. If mission controllers wanted the astronauts to change the shuttle's course or to test the robotic arm, Ride gave the message to the astronauts. Her expertise with the robotic arm helped her explain exactly what had to be done.

WHO GOES FIRST?

Before Ride joined NASA, only one woman had flown in space. Valentina Tereshkova of the Soviet Union (a nation from 1922 to 1991, based in modern-day Russia) orbited Earth for three days in 1963. In 1982, a second woman from the Soviet Union, Svetlana Savitskaya, orbited Earth for eight days.

Tereshkova prepares for liftoff in 1963.

NASA's first six female astronauts stand together at a press event in 1978.

Everyone at NASA wondered which of the six female astronauts would become the first American woman in space. All eyes would be on her. Some men at NASA thought that women didn't have the skills, strength, or smarts to fly into space. The first American woman in space had to prove them wrong.

On April 19, 1982, a NASA official gave Ride the news: she had been chosen to fly first. She had impressed her bosses and fellow astronauts with her work on the robotic arm and as a capsule communicator. She would train to fly on the space shuttle *Challenger*. It was scheduled for launch in June 1983.

WORLD OF WEIGHTLESSNESS

Astronauts need special tricks and tools to deal with weightlessness. They use Velcro to attach equipment to walls and cabinets. They eat sticky foods that won't float off spoons and drink from sealed containers using straws. To rest, they attach sleeping bags to the wall and climb inside. The toilets on spacecraft have tubes that suck up human waste. Astronauts can't take showers because the water would float around, so they wash with damp cloths.

SALLY IN THE SPOTLIGHT

To prepare for their flight, Ride and her crewmates practiced takeoffs, landings, and other procedures inside a **simulator**. This mock vehicle contained all the controls and monitors found in a real space shuttle. The astronauts also rode in an airplane that gave passengers the feeling of weightlessness. It helped them prepare for space, where there would be no **gravity**.

As the time for launch neared, the media focused on Ride. A reporter for *Time* magazine asked whether she cried when she encountered a problem. The reporter was implying that women weren't tough. Such questions frustrated Ride. At a press conference, she said, "It's time that people realized that women in this country can do any job that they want to do."

Ride and the *Challenger* crew prepare to board the shuttle on the morning of their liftoff.

UP AND AWAY

Finally, the big day arrived. On June 18, 1983, *Challenger* blasted off. About 200 miles (322 km) above Earth, the shuttle reached space and began to orbit the planet. Flying at 5 miles (8 km) per second, it would circle Earth sixteen times a day.

Inside, the astronauts experienced weightlessness. Without gravity, they simply floated around the shuttle. Sally thought floating was fun. She also loved seeing Earth from space. But the astronauts had work to do. They conducted several experiments, and they launched and captured satellites using the robotic arm.

After orbiting for a week, the shuttle headed back to Earth. The ride through the atmosphere was hot and bumpy. The shuttle glided to Earth like an airplane, landing at an air force base in California.

TECH TALK

"I wanted a competent engineer who was cool under stress. Sally had demonstrated that talent."

—Challenger *commander Robert Crippen, on why Ride became America's first woman in space*

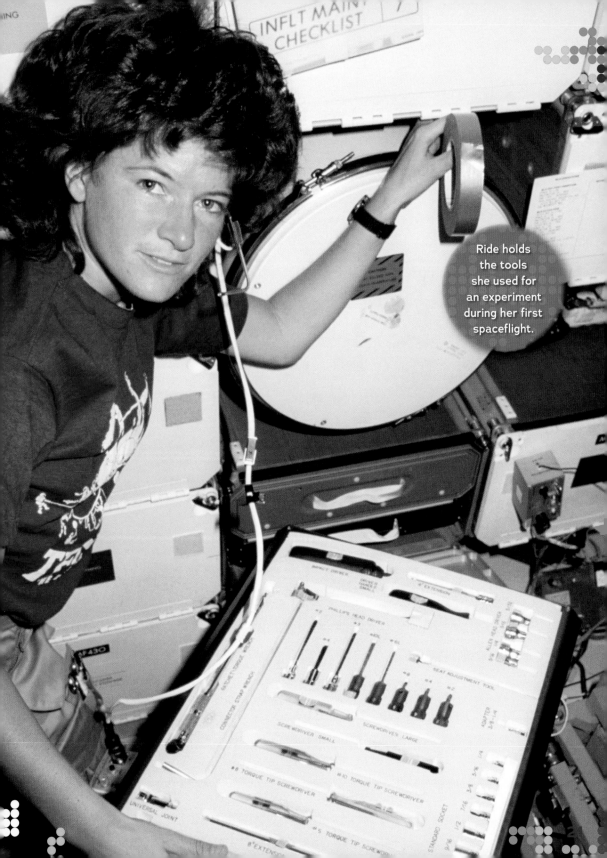

Ride holds the tools she used for an experiment during her first spaceflight.

Chapter 4

The *Challenger* crew during Ride's second flight

DOWN TO EARTH

The shuttle program continued carrying crews of astronauts into space. All six of the original female astronauts got their chances to fly. Ride flew on *Challenger* again in 1984. This was the first shuttle flight to include two women. During the eight-day mission, astronaut Kathryn

Sullivan became the first American woman to walk in space. Ride was scheduled for a third flight in July 1986, but in January, disaster struck. *Challenger* lifted off from the launchpad with a seven-member crew. About a minute later, the shuttle exploded. All the crew members died.

Ride was devastated by the death of her coworkers and friends. She joined a team of experts to investigate the disaster. The team uncovered the cause of the accident: faulty O-rings, or rubber seals, on the shuttle's launch rockets. Gas leaking through the seals had caused a fire. Sections of the shuttle started to burn. Then the whole craft exploded.

Gas and exhaust surrounded *Challenger* a few seconds after it exploded.

Ride speaks to a US government committee about science education.

BACK TO SCHOOL

In 1987, Ride retired from NASA. She became a physics professor at the University of California, San Diego, in 1989. But she wanted to teach younger students too. Studies showed that many kids began to lose interest in science in middle school. They started to think that scientists weren't cool. Ride wanted to change that. She wanted to get kids excited about science.

Along with her life partner, Tam O'Shaughnessy, Ride wrote books about space exploration for young readers. She also arranged for NASA to install a remotely controlled camera, called EarthKAM, on the space shuttle *Endeavour*. From their classrooms, students could control the camera and take pictures of Earth from space. After the International Space Station (ISS) began operations in 2000, she arranged to have EarthKAM moved to the ISS.

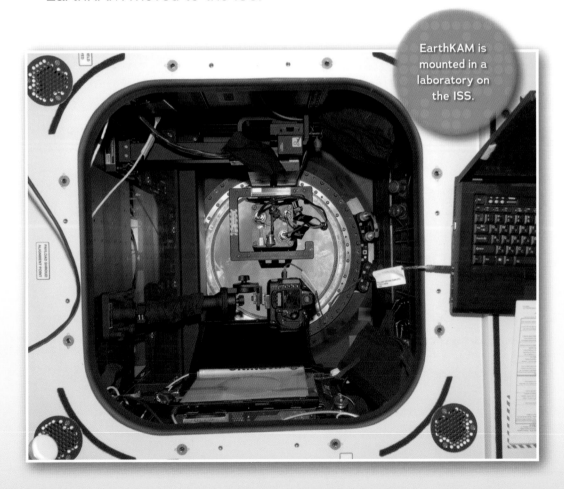

EarthKAM is mounted in a laboratory on the ISS.

TECH TALK

"Today we live in a world where little girls growing up realize that they can be astronauts or veterinarians or astrogeologists, and being able to put a female face on these careers can make all the difference."

—*Sally Ride, 2008*

In 2001, Ride and O'Shaughnessy founded a company called Sally Ride Science. The company wanted to encourage kids, especially girls, to pursue careers in science and math. It hosted science festivals, clubs, and camps and published kids' books about science. The company also made training materials for science teachers.

END OF THE LINE

Ride retired from teaching in 2007 and focused on Sally Ride Science full-time. In March 2011, she felt sick during a National Science Teachers Association conference. Her doctor discovered that she had pancreatic cancer. She underwent surgery and took chemotherapy and radiation treatments, but the cancer spread. Sally Ride died on July 23, 2012, at the age of sixty-one.

Every year, the president of the United States gives the Presidential Medal of Freedom to people who have made outstanding contributions to the United States. In 2013, Ride received the honor along with fifteen other Americans. Tam O'Shaughnessy accepted Ride's medal from President Barack Obama.

O'Shaughnessy stands with President Obama before accepting Ride's Presidential Medal of Freedom.

WOMEN IN SPACE

More than thirty years after Sally Ride's historic flight, female astronauts are common. Women have walked in space, piloted space shuttles, and commanded the ISS. By 2017, more than sixty women from many countries had flown in space.

Ride earned great fame in her life and inspired many. In 1983 the US Post Office created a Sally Ride stamp. Three US schools are named Sally Ride Elementary. A crater on the moon is also named for her. In 2014, the US Navy named a ship after her. As former NASA administrator Charles Bolden declared in 2013, "Dr. Sally Ride was more than an astronaut—she was an American treasure."

TIMELINE

1951

Sally Ride is born on May 26.

1962

John Glenn becomes the first American to orbit Earth.

1978

Ride receives her PhD from Stanford University and begins astronaut training.

1983

Ride becomes the first American woman to fly in space.

1986

Ride serves on a team investigating the space shuttle *Challenger* explosion.

1989

Ride becomes a professor of physics at the University of California, San Diego.

2001

Ride and Tam O'Shaughnessy found Sally Ride Science.

2003

Ride is inducted into the Astronaut Hall of Fame.

2012

Ride dies of pancreatic cancer.

2016

A ship named for Ride begins studying the life, water, and environment of the Pacific Ocean.

SOURCE NOTES

7 Lynn Sherr, *Sally Ride: America's First Woman in Space* (New York: Simon & Schuster, 2014), 27.

9 Ibid., 39.

19 "History in Five: Sally Ride, America's First Woman in Space," YouTube video, 7:18, posted by "Simon & Schuster Books," May 28, 2014, https://www.youtube.com /watch?v=jwu-zSdNiLI.

20 Michael Ryan, "A Ride in Space," *People*, June 20, 1983, http://people.com/archive /cover-story-a-ride-in-space-vol-19-no-24/.

26 "The Women's Conference 2006: Minerva Awards—Dr. Sally Ride," YouTube video, 8:30, posted by "thewomensconference," August 19, 2008, https://www.youtube .com/watch?v=GZX3LWrdMLU.

28 "President Obama Awards Presidential Medal of Freedom to Sally Ride," NASA, November 20, 2013, https://www.nasa.gov/content/president-obama-awards -presidential-medal-of-freedom-to-sally-ride/.

GLOSSARY

astrophysics
a branch of science that deals with the properties and behavior of stars, planets, galaxies, solar systems, and other objects and substances in space

atmosphere
the layer of gases surrounding Earth or another body in space

gravity
a force that pulls objects toward one another. Earth's gravity pulls objects toward the planet.

orbit
to travel around another object in a curved path

satellites
objects that orbit another object in space. Human-made satellites do such jobs as studying weather and relaying communications signals.

simulator
a model of a vehicle, outfitted with the same controls and systems found in the real vehicle

space shuttles
US space vehicles that flew between 1981 and 2011. The shuttles were carried into space by rockets and landed back on Earth like airplanes.

weightlessness
the feeling of not being pulled on by gravity

FURTHER
INFORMATION

BOOKS

Goldstein, Margaret J. *Astronauts: A Space Discovery Guide*.
Minneapolis: Lerner Publications, 2017.
Learn more about the work of astronauts, both on the ground and
when they're traveling on space missions.

Lassieur, Allison. *Astronaut Mae Jemison*. Minneapolis: Lerner
Publications, 2017.
Read all about Mae Jemison, a medical doctor who became NASA's
first black female astronaut.

O'Shaughnessy, Tam. *Sally Ride: A Photobiography of America's
Pioneering Woman in Space*. New York: Roaring Brook, 2015.
Check out this collection of personal photos and memories provided
by Sally Ride's friends and family.

WEBSITES

National Air and Space Museum
https://airandspace.si.edu
Browse this museum's website to find articles about Sally Ride
and other space pioneers, and lots more information about the US
space program.

Sally Ride Science
http://www.sallyridescience.com
Learn more about Ride's life and the work of her company, Sally
Ride Science.

INDEX

ABOUT THE AUTHOR

Margaret J. Goldstein, better known as Peg, was born in Detroit and attended the University of Michigan. For eight years, she worked in-house at Lerner Publications in Minneapolis, until she could no longer endure the 23-below-zero weather. She now lives in Palm Springs, California, where temperatures routinely top 100. She works as a freelance editor and writes books for young readers.

Mm Mm Mm Mm

Mm Mm Mm

Yum Yum Yum

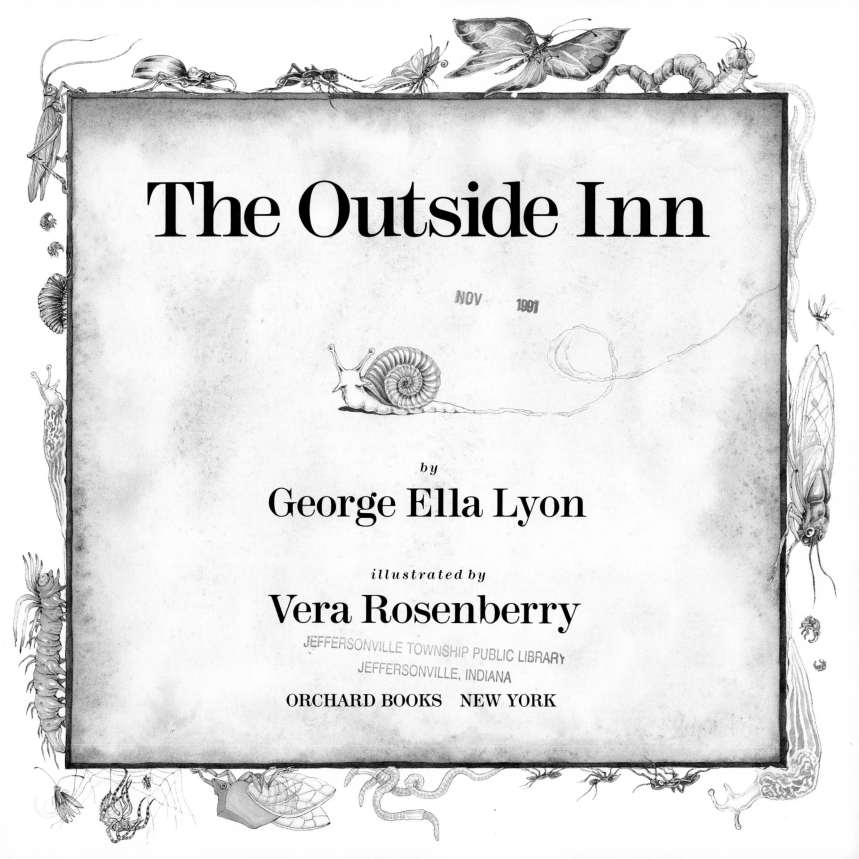

The Outside Inn

by

George Ella Lyon

illustrated by

Vera Rosenberry

ORCHARD BOOKS   NEW YORK

Text copyright © 1991 by George Ella Lyon
Illustrations copyright © 1991 by Vera Rosenberry

Orchard Books, A division of Franklin Watts, Inc.
387 Park Avenue South, New York, NY 10016

Manufactured in the United States of America. Printed by General Offset
Company, Inc. Bound by Horowitz/Rae. Book design by Mina Greenstein.
The text of this book is set in 36 pt. ITC Modern No. 216 Medium.
The illustrations are watercolor and ink line, done by brush, and
reproduced in full color.

10 9 8 7 6 5 4 3 2 1

Library of Congress Cataloging-in-Publication Data
Lyon, George Ella, date.
The Outside Inn / by George Ella Lyon ;
illustrations by Vera Rosenberry.   p.   cm.
Summary: The rhyming verse presents all sorts of "appetizing" meals to
be had outdoors, including "puddle ink to drink," "gravel crunch for
lunch," and "worms and dirt for dessert."
ISBN 0-531-05936-7 (trade).   ISBN 0-531-08536-8 (lib.)
[1. Stories in rhyme.   2. Humorous stories.]
I. Rosenberry, Vera, ill.   II. Title.
PZ8.3.L9893Ou   1991   [E]—dc20   90-14285

For Kathleen Sterling
poet, teacher, friend

—G.E.L.

For Raman —V.R.

Welcome to The Outside Inn
where good times and good food begin.
What'll you have? What'll it be?
I'm your waiter. Just ask me.

What's for breakfast?

Ants

with

ketchup.

What's to drink?

Puddle ink.

What's for snack?

Slugs in a sack.

What's for lunch?

Gravel crunch.

What's for treat?

Caterpillar feet.

What's for tea?

A
sowbug
and
a flea.

Yum Yum

Yum Yum.

What's for dinner?

Mud-pie thinner.

What's
for
dessert?

Worms
and
dirt.

WORMS

and

DIRT

? ? ?

Squirm in your spoon
and **wriggle** at your chin.
Meals that crawl
from The Outside Inn!

Mm Mm Mm

Yum Yum Yum